For there to be true change in the church. . .we must move

BEYOND RADICAL

BE WARNED: THIS MAY WELL BE THE MOST REVOLUTIONARY PIECE OF CHRISTIAN LITERATURE YOU WILL EVER READ.

BEYOND
RADICAL

by
Gene
Edwards

Cover design by Jenny Jeffries.

Library of Congress Cataloging-in-Publication Data

Edwards, Gene
      Beyond Radical/Gene Edwards.
      ISBN 0-930232-70-7
      1. Christian books-non-fiction

Printed in the United States of America

THIS IS A CALL
TO BREAK WITH THE PRESENT
PRACTICE OF CHRISTIANITY
IN A WAY MORE RADICAL
THAN WAS KNOWN DURING
THE PROTESTANT
REFORMATION

THERE IS NO SCRIPTURAL
GROUND
FOR ANYTHING
WE PROTESTANTS PRACTICE.

AS YOU WILL NOW SEE. . .

You are about to read a list of very familiar practices, rituals, etc., which we evangelicals participate in every week.

All these practices came into the Christian faith long *after* the first century.

* * *

Most of the things we Protestants practice had their beginnings long after the first century. None of them began with any thought of being scriptural. *No one* was thinking of the Word of God when they started these practices.

After you have read where these practices began and how not-in-scripture they are, if you then want to return to first-century ways, you will have to move

BEYOND RADICAL.

Here is the list.

What We Do That Is Not Scriptural

THE CHURCH BUILDING

PASTORS

THE ORDER OF WORSHIP

THE SERMON

THE PULPIT

THE PEW

THE CHOIR

CHAPTER AND VERSE

Reading Scripture just before the sermon

THE FUNERAL

THE FUNERAL ORATION

SUNDAY SCHOOL

The Order in Which Paul's Letters Are Arranged in the New Testament

THE SEMINARY

THE BIBLE SCHOOL

INTERDENOMINATIONAL AND PARA-CHURCH ORGANIZATIONS

THE MATTER OF ALL PROTESTANTS GOING TO CHURCH ON SUNDAY AT 10 OR 11 A.M.

THE ALTAR CALL

Hold on to your hat, because everything on this list is defended as being "clearly taught in the Word of God." But every practice on that list started in very strange ways, and long after the first century. Now, today, for some odd reason, we have managed to find every one of them in the Scripture!

Finding out where these practices came from may help you understand why we are in the mess we are in. After that you must face another question.

What question?

One which will spring up from your own heart.

1

The Story Behind
What We Do

We will start by finding out why it is that all of us Christians "go to church" on Sunday. And at 11 a.m.

Always having "church" at 11 a.m. Sunday morning was started by Martin Luther. He drank an awful lot of beer on Saturday night at the local pub. The older he got, the longer he stayed at the pub, and consequently, the later he had to set the morning church service. Today 500,000,000 Protestants routinely (and without question) follow this Sunday tradition because of the beer-drinking habits of a German theologian.

The Pastor

Think about it. Where in the New Testament do you find a man—the same man—who (1) preaches every Sunday, (2) marries people, (3) brings a message over a corpse, then (4) buries it with a prayer, (5) visits old ladies, (6) says prayers over football games, (7) CEO's a church, (8) presides over elders and deacons, (9) is virtually always in a dress suit, (10) speaks strangely and prays funny, (11) baptizes all the new converts, and (12) whose office and all the above practices are supposed to be based solidly on the Word of God and found in Scripture.

Such a man is not there in your New Testament is he? Yet, today, the man is the central figure in Protestant Christianity. Just how did the pastor idea get into Christianity? Here is the story. See for yourself if it sounds like it sprang out of "solidly based on the Word of God."

Pope Gregory the Great first popularized the term "pastor" in about 550 A.D. He did so by writing a book on the *pastoral* duties of the *priest*! The term *pastor* appears in no Christian literature before that point other than once in a long list of people mentioned in the book of Ephesians. The practical meaning of the word is unknown.

Pope Gregory told Roman Catholic *priests* to carry out *pastoral* duties: to visit the sick, teach doctrine, marry the young, sprinkle the babies, conduct the Mass, bury the dead, and bless local events (such as festivals). These became forever the Roman Catholic priest's *pastoral duties*. No such man and no such duties ever existed in Scripture.

Luther came along a thousand years later and slightly altered this list of *pastoral* duties for Lutheran priests. Gradually the term *pastor* emerged into Protestant vocabulary throughout the English speaking world. The word pastor replaced the Catholic term *priest*. The man does not exist in first-century literature. Neither do these *practices* exist in the New Testament.

We Anglos carried this pastor idea, which Luther invented, to the ends of the earth. It is now Christianity.

If we removed the present pastoral role from Christendom, there would be an almost total collapse of "church" worldwide. Yet the present pastoral practice has absolutely no scriptural grounds. Try to find this man in the first century. If we move away from the pastor being center, we move beyond radical.

Church Buildings

Until a Roman emperor named Constantine came along (about 300 years after Pentecost), the Christian faith was the only religion in history that met in homes. It was the only "lay" led movement in the history of religion. Christianity alone had no institutions, no set rituals, no temples. That was unprecedented in human history. It is what made Christianity unique. And virile. And elastic, flexible, and adaptable. It had low overheads! Costs were minimal. Constantine changed all that.

All other religions of mankind had these
elements:

temples

priests

vestal virgins

ritual

*a secret vocabulary understood only by the
    priest*

a silent laity.

Look at that list again. Christianity now has all
of these. (Okay, we Protestants do not have vestal
virgins!)

In the year 327 A.D. (mark that date, as it is
pivotal in Christian history) Constantine ordered the
construction of nineteen Christian buildings. That
had never happened before. Until then, we met in
homes. (At first, buildings were seen as shrines.)

These nineteen buildings were constructed in
three places. *One* in Bethlehem and *two* in Jerusalem
(for His birth, crucifixion and resurrection), nine in
the city of Constantinople and seven in the city of
Rome.

Constantine primarily launched these buildings
for his brand new city in the east. It was a custom-
made city, created from he dirt up. The city was
uninhabited   until   it   was   completed
. . .with empty streets, grand government buildings,
and the nine Christian buildings scattered around
the city. The city also had an abundance of pagan
temples. These were named after a god or a

goddess. Constantine, a pagan in mind if not in soul, therefore ordered that each one to the nine Christian buildings be named after *someone*. Specifically they were to be named after first-century saints! (Hence: St. Luke's church, St. John's church, etc. Yep! That is how it began.)

In Rome, the same year, Constantine ordered the construction of seven Christian buildings. (One was a shrine placed on the side of a hill just outside the city walls. The slope of the hill was called Vaticanus.)

That is how (the curse of) the church building began.

Very scriptural, we Bible-practicing Protestants, are we not?

These buildings later came to be known as churches. So it came about that Christianity joined all the other religions of the world and came to have its very own temples. The effect of these buildings was that we drifted further away from the spirit that had permeated the primeval Christian community. Why this should be so becomes clear when we consider that our word church has no equivalent in the original New Testament. The word church goes back to the Greek *kyriakon*, belonging to the Lord, which was understood to mean *house belonging to the Lord*. Later the meaning was extended to refer to the people who gathered in a particular locale as well as to whole denominations (e.g. Church of England). The New Testament, however, knows only the Ekklesia, the community of the saints. She is the house of the Lord, built of living stones. With the word *church* our eyes were turned away from the living ekklesia of the living God to a dead edifice made of dead stones. (Even our creeds that define our denominations are nothing but dead letters.) The damage that was done will never be redressed. Any hope of a true grasp of ecclesiology died not long after Constantine died in 337 A.D.

Following the introduction of the temple into our faith, there came the secret language, the remote priest, the silent followers, the rituals, and the vestal virgins.

The loss for all of us has been staggering. These things we acquired have been a curse for the simple faith Jesus the carpenter launched.

The Pew

When the Italian Christians walked into these shiny new buildings which were built in Rome and when the Greeks walked into the buildings in Constantinople, they discovered there was nowhere to sit down. The Italians dragged in three-legged stools and sat down!

On the other hand, when the Christians in Constantinople walked into these shiny new buildings, something odd happened. Someone demanded that, out of respect for Christ, everyone should stand. (The name of the man who did this odd thing is lost to us.) No sitting. No stools.

Stand! The result? Today the Eastern Orthodox churches still have no place to sit down in their churches. . .despite the fact their Sunday ritual is two hours long! Unto this day they have no pews, and scarcely any windows. No wonder the devout Eastern Orthodox church did not grow like Roman Catholicism!

(By the way, later the Roman Catholics replaced the three-legged stool with the bench.)

Just before the Protestant Reformation, someone figured out how to put a back on a bench. So was born both the chair and the bench with a back. The Protestants jumped on the idea, and so was born the Protestant pew. Grumblingly, the Catholics of Western Europe are gradually taking out the bench and putting in the pew. (In America, almost from the beginning, the Catholics capitulated to the pew, to compete with the Protestants.)

It was not until the arrival of the enlightened minds of us twentieth-century evangelicals that we got really New Testament and put cushions on our pews. (This way we can at least be comfortable while being bored to death.)

The pew's future? In our electronic age, perhaps we will see vibrating back rubs? Electric finger massages? Stereophonic earphones to better hear the choir? Who knows!

One thing is sure: "Church" will always be a building, and meeting in houses as the ekklesia is never going to be *the* place Christians gather.

The Choir

Yes, the term is used in the Old Testament. But by no means can we justify the choir because of that fact. Historically the choir you find in a Christian church has its roots straight out of pagan choirs that were present in heathen temples. The Christian choir first appeared in Christian buildings commissioned by Constantine. None existed before Constantine. As the church building fad moved across Europe, the choir became universal. Future choirs were patterned after the choir in Milan, Italy, circa 400 A.D. where the choir was perfected under the leadership of a bishop named Ambrose.

The Pulpit

The pulpit predates Christianity and is of heathen origin. The heathen priest, standing in a heathen temple, moved out onto a walkway which had a banister around it and made his announcements to the pagan onlookers. This arrangement, by which the priest was separated from the people, was called *ambo*. The word or a similar one expressing that separation can be found in most European languages.*

The first Christian church buildings, the basilicas, were also furnished with this heathen arrangement, except that it was now inside the building. It was a platform with a banister around it and it had two elevated parts (the ambos). These ambos, one of which was higher than the other, were used to read from the Gospels and Epistles respectively, but in some instances they were used to make a distinction between a mere reader and a speaker.

In the eleventh century it became customary to build only one ambo, which was elevated on a pillar. This is the pulpit with which we are familiar.

Centuries later, when the Protestants took over Northern Europe (by the sword, not by evangelizing), those Protestants inherited thousands upon thousands of Catholic church buildings. In many places they tore out that unapproachable area up front where the priests had conducted their magical mass. But change did not stop there. Especially in modern times, the ambo was taken down from its pillar and placed in front, either to the side or in the center. In churches that do not have an altar, the pulpit is always centered and has a large Bible on it to symbolize the centrality of preaching the Bible as over against the Catholic central emphasis on the Mass.

For instance, the lectern in the Roman Catholic church (still a sort of second ambo which Lutherans also use) is called Ambo *in German. Our English* pulpit, *and the Italian* pulpito, *are derived from the late Latin* pulpitum *which referred to an elevated platform for performers. The German* kanzel *(pulpit), as the English* chancel, *derives from late Latin* cancellus *(lattice) and signifies something fenced off. The French word for pulpit* la chaire, *goes back to the Latin* cathedra *which took on the meaning of chair in the sense of "position to teach with authority." It is clear that all these words express separation from the ordinary members, and represent an idea foreign to the primeval church.*

The Sermon

Not to be confused with a Christian message. It is true there may at first seem to be only a slight difference, but that difference is really gigantic.

Long before Christianity came into existence, a heathen philosopher, Aristotle by name, teaching on many subjects, taught on the subject of *rhetoric*— that is, how to bring an oration. (Greek: retorike . . .the art of the orator) Speechmaking had been the great love of the Greeks before Aristotle. He raised it to an art form.

In the days of the Greeks and Romans, the ability to bring a great oration was a guarantee of popularity. Great orators were actually the *movie stars* of that day.

Aristotle's discourse on rhetoric covered many things about speechmaking, but his main point was that a good speech must have: (1) a clear introduction, (2) a few major points and (3) a conclusion.

No such ideas existed among the early believers. First-century believers, being almost universally illiterate, knew no such thing as the rules of speechmaking. First-century Christian preaching was characterized by being extemporaneous, spontaneous, and urgent. . .and it belonged to the entire body of believers, not to a special class of men!

The sermons you hear every week are based on Aristotle's concepts of oration. (Often seminary professors who teach the art of the sermon know nothing of these facts.)

Now how did heathen speechmaking ever manage to get into the Christian faith?

In Antioch, Syria, circa 400 A.D., one of the great heathen orators of all time, John Chrysostom (John the Goldenmouth) became a believer. He brought his Aristotelian rhetoric/sermon skills into Christianity. He quickly rocketed his way into being the leading priest in Antioch and in all Syria. The whole city of Antioch turned out to hear his orations. Those messages sound *very* similar to great heathen speeches in style, delivery, structure *and*—to some degree—even content. (So also did the sermon you heard last Sunday.)

It is John Chrysostom who not only gave us Aristotelian sermonics, but also gave us the custom of the *Sunday morning* sermon, that is, the tradition of a Sunday oration being delivered by the same man, in the same place, at the same time, *every* Sunday.

Hence you see the origin of the sermon and the Sunday church services. But John Chrysostom also gave the Catholic priests one of their "pastoral duties." The custom of teaching evolved along the way, until today teaching is the central duty of the Protestant pastor. Protestant pastors have no idea they are carrying out a modified version of the seven major *pastoral* duties of a priest.

Truly, then, here is a large hunk of the pastoral

role—one man—the same man—sermonizing us every Sunday. Remember these origins next Sunday.

The Sunday sermon is the only place left on earth where you can hear an oratory delivered in the grand Greek/Roman tradition of rhetoric!

True to the New Testament and nothing but the New Testament, huh, fellow evangelicals?

Funerals

Because John Chrysostom as a heathen had long practiced the heathen custom of bringing a pagan oration over the dead, he continued this practice when he became a Christian orator. So began the "Christian" funeral and the funeral oration that goes with it. Words we use when preaching over the Christian dead are almost word for word the typical heathen orations given over the heathen dead. Read a pagan philosopher's funeral oration. Read a John Chrysostom funeral oration. Hear a Christian funeral sermon. They are virtually the same in their general content, and very much the same in the style of delivery. (Very New Testament, we evangelicals.)

The Practice of Reading Scripture Before a Sermon

This practice is so much a part of our lives we can hardly imagine beginning a Christian message or hearing a Christian message any other way. It is still heathen in origin! When the pagan orator stepped out upon the stage of a Greek amphitheater, he went through a rather odd (but recognizable) ritual.

The orator first walked to the center of the stage, turned his back on the audience, and draped an orator's gown about him. He then turned, faced the audience and opened a scroll.

A scroll? Yes, a book. What book? Usually it would be one of the writings of the author Homer or some other well-known Greek writer.

That is not all. The writings of Homer and other popular writers of Greek/Roman literature had been meticulously divided into chapters! Each chapter had a number. Each sentence in that chapter also had a number!

This pagan practice was carried over into the Christian faith. Dividing the New Testament into chapters and verses grew out of a Greco/Roman practice. So did the practice of reading a passage of Scripture *before* preaching a sermon. All of this got into the Christian faith from around 400 A.D. to 500 A.D.

Try bringing a message today from a heathen-rooted pulpit, with the heathen concept of a choir behind you, and a mute laity sitting on heathen-inspired pews. Then, doing all that, try preaching without first reading chapter and verse from the New Testament.

In some churches, the people would get up and leave the (heathen-inspired building called a) church because *you* were not being really scriptural before you preached your Greco-influenced oratorical sermon, without first reading a passage of Scripture.

The practice of reading Scriptures before a sermon finds its roots in the Greek habit of heathenism's orations delivered in Grecian amphitheaters.

Think about it, dear student of the Bible!

What dare we say of chapter and verse? One day our children may say it was perhaps the greatest damage of all. Why? This heathen practice of chopping up living letters into numbered chapters and numbered sentences caused us to lose the whole first-century flavor of first-century Christian literature.

*   *   *

Let us pause for a moment and catch our breath. It has been wisely said the problems of the Protestant and evangelical faith are not in its teachings and doctrines, but in its practice.

Our evangelical practices came to us by pure accident. They bear no relationship to the first-century Christian experience. Most of our practices (1) are by happenstance, (2) are heathen in origin, (3) started around the time of Constantine and/or during the Reformation.

Virtually every practice we have today came from an accident of church history or from heathenism.

Just think. You have been doing all these things ever since you got saved.

Anyone for revolution?

Let us continue our search for the true historical roots of our evangelical practices. *It gets worse! Much worse!*

2

Some of the Big Ones

It is amazing what we do—and how many things we do—which have no New Testament justification, yet are defended as being "New Testament." These totally unscriptural (even harmful) practices are done in the midst of a daily cry of: "We must be biblical." "We must be New Testament." "We must be true to the Word of God."

This is really scary. Our practices are heathen-rooted, yet we somehow manage to find these practices in the New Testament. That, dear reader, is *really* scary. We can find *all these things* in the New Testament!

Oh, they are not there, but we can find them there.

You have seen the list of our Protestant practices. That list covers just about everything we Protestants do. May you be shaken to the roots of your being as you see where all these "scriptural" things really come from. But more importantly, what is going on in our evangelical brain which allows us to find these things in Scripture? What mindset allows such insanity?

Such things as:

Seminaries

Seminaries are the heart of where we learn the Word of God. It is there we are taught "faithfulness to the Word of God." "We need to be New Testament." And "Let's get back to the Bible." But ask any seminary professor: Where did seminaries originate? He probably has no idea. (For goodness sake, never ask him if they are scriptural! And never ask him to lead the charge to end them.)

Where did seminaries come from? They are in the Bible?

No, the Catholics invented them.

Where?

Just south of the Italian border.

When?

At a council called by the Pope. The purpose of the council was to figure out how to countermand Martin Luther and his reformation. These men were deciding whether or not to reform the Roman Catholic church or stay as they were. Even though it lasted eighteen years, almost nothing came out of that council except the invention of seminaries. The Council of Trent lasted from 1545 to 1563 and was attended by bishops, cardinals and popes. The idea of seminaries was thought up near the close of this council (January 1562—December 1563).

The curriculum which is followed in seminaries (which Protestants began to establish soon after the Catholics invented it) actually followed the curriculum used in the universities which first emerged during the Middle Ages. Theology was the core curriculum of the early universities.

The Council of Trent deemed it wise to separate clergy training from the universities. It still kept a curriculum set in the Platonic and Aristotelian model.

The Bible School

In the late 1800's, a man named D.L. Moody considered it unnecessary for a Christian to have to go all the way through university before entering seminary. He, therefore, invented the first *Bible school*, located in Chicago. (This allowed young men and women to go directly out of high school into theological training.)

Nevertheless, the Bible schools also followed the Catholic-Protestant curriculum which had been developed by the European Universities. But these universities, which began to flourish between 1100 and 1550, were in turn patterned after Aristotle's academia of the 4th century B.C.

The Sunday School

Our nation is filled with costly Sunday school

buildings. Very costly! The many, many rooms in these buildings are used only two hours a week and remain empty during the other 166 hours of the week! They are the most unused buildings ever erected by mankind (exceeding even the church building in *non-use*.) In the late 1800's D.L.Moody brought the Sunday school to America from England. Sunday schools were invented over 1700 years after the New Testament closed. Yet, today, we some way manage to find the Sunday school on every page of the New Testament.

By the way, ask any child if he *really* likes going to Sunday school. . .or church.

The Nonprofit Interdenominational, Tax-Exempt, Nondenominational Para-Church Organization

When and where did the para-church organization begin?

John R. Mott and D.L.Moody began the first two significant para-church organizations: the YMCA and the Student Volunteer Movement. Today, there are thousands of "non-church" organizations.

If the truth be known, virtually all these organizations are created to circumvent "church." They exist to fill in the holes church has left empty. Not-a-church organizations exist in the presence of the failing of the present-day practice of church. Today there are more para-church and non-church movements with more *staff* (that is, more ministers and missionaries)—and more spendable money than all the evangelical churches combined have. Yet the para-church concept started less than 150 years ago.

Most interesting of all, ever since these organizations began to receive acceptance (about 1950), they also have suddenly been discovered to be *in* the New Testament.

Such is the capacity of our present Protestant and evangelical mindset: to find *all* the things we do in the New Testament which were never in the New Testament until after we invented them. . .*then* they were found in the New Testament.

Anyone for being New Testament?

Now We Come To One of the Biggest and Baddest

The Sunday Morning Protestant Ritual—that is, the Sunday "order of worship."

Wherever you "go to church" next Sunday, note the order of worship. Regardless of your denomination, it will follow this pattern:

> *two songs*
> *a prayer*
> *two more songs*
> *the offering*
> *a prayer*
> probably special music by the choir,
> *or a solo*

then the sermon (Remember, that sermon is basically based on a Greco-Roman oration.)

Finally, the benediction

Where did this ritual come from? Did Paul give it to us? Peter? Can you find it anywhere in the New Testament? (Try comparing this iron-cast ritual to I Corinthians 14.)

As you walk out of the church building, think about this: Some five hundred million (500,000,000) Protestants will go through exactly that same ritual. Every week! All over the world. Forever. Next week in the jungles of Borneo, the jungles of Africa, the jungles of South America. The Eskimos. The Arabs. The Japanese. The Mongolians. *All* will follow this same "order of worship"!

And all will be bored.

Missionaries from Britain and America have imposed this ritual on all the Protestants now residing on this planet. Some 500,000,000 of us have had this abominable ritual imposed on us. (A pox on you folks who did this to us. But you have been punished! You had to sit through this ritual yourself!)

Dare we justify the *order of worship* as being scriptural?

Basically, today, Christianity *is* this ritual. This ritual defines all that unbelievers across this entire planet know us by.

We have reached a point where this Sunday morning ritual has literally "evangelized the world."

It is the only way Protestants meet! Any other way of meeting, any other way of assembling. . .in any other place but a building. . .is simply not conceived. It would be an act of heresy to have a meeting being led by someone who is not a minister, or being led by no one at all, and, on top of that. . .shudder. . . not following any order at all.

Yet this universal Sunday ritual we all sit through has not a shred of New Testament ground to justify itself. In fact, this ritual flies in the face of first-century ways.

This perfunctory ritual is also one of the greatest stumbling blocks in Christianity to its vitality and variety. In fact, this Sunday ritual—and all its trappings—is killing us. In every generation, for five hundred years, this Protestant ritual has been choking the life out of the Christian faith.

Who is responsible for strangling the Christian faith with this "Sunday service?" Who invented the Sunday church service ritual?

The inventor of this hour of unrelenting boredom was John Calvin. About 1540. In Geneva, Switzerland. Add it up. That is almost 1400 years *after* the first century. And we will never recover from this invention. Not ever! This ritual will prevail—in church buildings—on Sunday—at 11 a.m.—until the end of this creation.

Thousands of profound books on liturgy have proven beyond all doubt that this ritual, invented in circa 1540, is *the way* Christians in the first century met and worshipped. Yes, we now find John Calvin's ritual *in* the New Testament.

A call to revolution!

If this is not enough to edge you into new realms, try the next one, because it may be the most serious mess of all.

3

The Worst Disaster of All

It is virtually impossible to really understand what the New Testament is saying and why. That is because (1) we approach it wrongly; and (2) in your New Testament Paul's letters are not arranged in the order they should be. Change these two facts and we will all see a revolution. Change these two facts and find yourself in a thrilling new relationship to your New Testament.

You will find yourself in for a *spiritual* revolution *and* a revolution of church *practice*.

Could that really be important? Yes, the future of Christendom hangs on breaking with the present tradition of arranging Paul's letters the way they are arranged in the New Testament. We desperately need a New Testament with Paul's letters arranged in the order in which he wrote them.

The *first* letter Paul wrote was not Romans. In your New Testament the first letter Paul wrote finds itself appearing as the *fourth* letter. In your New Testament, all of his letters are out of their chronological order. If this goes on forever, we will forever be kept from understanding the New Testament!

Repeat: A major reason we are in the mess we are in is the way we are taught the New Testament. Learning the New Testament the way we presently learn the New Testament is what keeps us from ever learning the New Testament.

To illustrate, imagine this.

Here is a nine-volume set of books on mathematics. But the books are never read in order. Imagine this is also true of a nine-volume set of books on electricity, on physics, on astronomy etc. All these nine-volume sets have the same problem. None of the books are in their proper sequence! Also, imagine that everyone studies these books in their jumbled-up order.

Would you ever learn math this way? Try. Here is what you are up against. The first book that you come to is actually Volume Six, the next one you come to is Volume Four, then Volume Five, then, finally, Volume One, and after that Volume Eight, then. . .etc.

Can you ever understand mathematics that way? Or electrons, *or* Scripture?

Well, that is exactly the jumbled-up sequence Paul's letters are put in right now. . .6, 4, 5, 1, etc.

. . .in every New Testament in print in every language on earth.

Romans is Paul's sixth letter. I Corinthians, his fourth. II Corinthians, his fifth. Galatians, his first, etc.

"We will preach through the New Testament." "We will study the New Testament."

In so doing, we *think* we will learn the New Testament. But chaos greets us when we come to the letters Paul wrote to the churches.

"Our Bible school teaches all the books in the New Testament."

But even in the most scholarly seminaries on earth, the letters Paul wrote to churches are taught in this present chaotic order.

Try learning history in a nine-volume set arranged in this order: 6, 4, 5, 1, 8, 10, 7, 2, 3, 11, 13, 12, 9. Well, this *is* the order in which Paul's letters appear in your New Testament.

No one can ever know what these nine books say until they are read in chronological sequence.

Long ago we abandoned any concept of seeing the actual story of the first century. Long ago we abandoned the idea of seeing the letters of Paul in the totality of their original setting. In such a chopped-up setting, never seeing the sequence of events, never knowing the story, all of us are left in the dark as to what the New Testament is revealing. Total contextuality—that is, seeing the entire setting—is not, and never has been, a factor in New Testament studying.

The story. . .*the* story. . .is neither taught nor known. Not by laymen, *not* by scholars.

Not known, not taught, not learned, not even an awareness of the lack. Most of all, never realizing the greater catastrophic problems created by not knowing *the story*.

The consequence of not being able to follow the story brings us to the other great tragedy which prevents us from knowing the New Testament: the way we approach the New Testament.

For 500 years Protestantism has had a field day with *verses!* That is. . .with sentences. *Numbered* sentences. No one has had to deal with the *constraints* of the immovable *story*. Contrariwise, we have created havoc with those very movable verses!

We can prove anything with numbered sentences.

We could not do that if we knew *the story*.

Total contextuality is unknown.

Chronological exposition is unknown.

New Testament Bible study by a timeline is unknown.

The result: *The story* is utterly unknown.

Yet, if you come to know the story *first*, you must then abandon virtually all the present practices of Protestantism. They were built by verses. If we knew the story first, we would either change, or live the rest of our Christian life knowing we were living outside the practice of the church first-century style. These present practices of ours can find no justification for existence within *the story*. The entire story renders our present Protestant methods utterly unjustifiable.

Paul's first epistle was Galatians. His second letter was to the church in Thessalonica. There was a great deal which happened before the Galatian letter was written. Do you know *that part* of the story?

About nine months passed between the time Paul wrote Galatians and I Thessalonians.

A lot happened in between the writing of those two letters.

Do you know what happened during those nine months? Do you know that part of the story? Does anybody? Does anybody care? It is time for us to care, to learn, to know. We so desperately need to know the story—the *whole* story, from beginning to end.

About three months passed between I Thessalonians and the writing of II Thessalonians. An awful lot happened in between. Does anybody know the story of what happened between those two letters?

Do you?

The next letter Paul wrote was to Corinth. But there are six years between II Thessalonians and the

45

first letter to Corinth. Six years. Do you know what happened during those years? Does anybody know *that* part of the story?

The fact that no New Testament has ever appeared in the English language with Paul's letters in their proper order is proof enough that we are blind to the story—unaware of the power of that story and the importance of that story.

The story binds us to *reality.* It renders *verses* almost powerless. We have never thought in terms of knowing the New Testament chronologically or learning it "story wise" and "story first." We are so fascinated with numbered sentences which we call verses that we never realize there is a story.

The story tells us the *real* meaning—and the limits—of those verses. Remove the safeguard of knowing the story and no one will ever *know* the New Testament, and we will continue proving anything and everything by verses. Remove the safeguard of the story—the whole story—and you can prove any idea you fancy and create any theory you wish. The story limits just how many air castles we can build with all those verses!

Step one in learning the story is to learn the proper chronological sequence of Paul's letters:

Galatians
I Thessalonians
II Thessalonians
I Corinthians
II Corinthians

Romans
Colossians
Ephesians
Philemon
Philippians
I Timothy
Titus
II Timothy

Learning that story will humble us all. Then learn the whole story.

Consider this: Take away these Protestant practices of ours and the entire Protestant mindset crumbles. The very mindset collapses!

Do you now glimpse the insane results of this insane neglect?

For 500 years we have never taught the entire— very dramatic—story, in its entirety, not from one end to the other in dramatic, chronological order. As a result, with all vaunted schools and endless books, even seminary professors with several doctorate degrees *cannot* tell you that story.

It is not known.

Bible teachers do not know the story.

Sunday school teachers do not.

Pastors do not.

The results: a field day for every conceivable idea the mind of man can dream up. Numbered sentences which you can move around allow *anything*.

Knowing that very knowable *story* puts a stop to such insanity.

Until we know the story we cannot know the Scripture.

Unnerving isn't it?

Why have we not considered something as simple as reading Scripture in the way it was chronologically written and including the historical facts to fill in the gaps between books, thereby learning *the story*?

Read the Scriptures in this new way and see if you do not discover a brand new Bible. Then again, maybe you had better never learn that story. It might be hazardous to your present Christian practices!

Lacking that story, we have moved our entire mindset of "learning the Bible" into the never-never land of sewing together disjointed verses and calling that "Bible study." We even dare call this practice *scholarship*! Without the story, that which we call *theology* is both dangerous and—if you can follow the thought—*unscriptural*. Verses do not make for scriptural soundness. We have confined ourselves to reading *our* "math," *our* "astrophysics," *our* New Testament, from the mountain of chaos.

We have thirteen letters of Paul, nine to churches and four to friends. We find them in this very chaotic and non-chronological order:

Romans
I Corinthians
II Corinthians

Galatians
Ephesians
Philippians
Colossians
I Thessalonians
II Thessalonians
I Timothy
II Timothy
Titus
Philemon

So you thought you knew the New Testament!! None of us ever will unless we know and appreciate (1) the story and (2) the chronology.

Find the order of these letters. Find the story of what happened in between. Then keep a clear conscience. Do that, and you will move *beyond* radical.*

You can memorize the entire New Testament (in Greek) and still have no idea what the New Testament is saying! Not if you memorize it in the present non-story, non-chronological, chaotic order. The mindset with which we come to the New Testament renders us impotent to see the first-century setting. Verses, teachings, doctrines, ideals, schemes, and most of all, justification of our view, crowd out the story. We can say, "This came from

---

You may receive a free audio tape entitled "Why We Do Not Know What the New Testament Says," *by writing for it at the SeedSowers address.*

the Word of God," no matter how pea-brained the idea we come up with.

Knowing the story tames such a mindset.

To illustrate:

Many a man has read through the New Testament and decided what God wants— "based on clear biblical teaching."

Let us say that he decides that what God wants a people to do is move out into the wilderness, far from the world, live righteous lives, breathe pure air, grow organic food, wear old style country clothes and stay away from the world ("the organic carrot juice syndrome" blended with the "Essene syndrome"). A man can justify every one of those proton-sized ideas with "the pure Word of God."

But! If that man and his listeners knew *the story*—the whole story of the first century—he would not have an organic vegetable to stand on, and his listeners would head for the door. *The story* allows no such fantasies as he preaches.

How badly do we need to know the story, the whole story? Consider this:

Christians have fought and massacred one another for centuries. . .with verses. . .never knowing *the story*.

A whole revolution in scriptural understanding awaits us if we dare learn the story.

Now, here is a question of questions. How did the New Testament books ever get placed in this jumbled-up order? Who cursed us with the present arrangement of the books in the New Testament?

Once more: Luther. (He never knew the story of what happened in the first century. He never knew what happened in between the letters Paul wrote. But, boy oh boy, did he know verses!)

The fellow who started this chaotic mess was the man who produced the very *first* Protestant Bible. All the versions of the Bible since then have followed his model. All New Testaments start Paul's letters with his letter to the Romans. The first Protestant Bible was the work of Martin Luther. Consequently, he was also the one who arranged the order of Paul's letters. Luther was an Augustinian monk who taught dogmatic theology in a university town called Wittenburg, located in Eastern Germany. He taught Paul's letters. . .from the viewpoint of doctrine. *Only* doctrine. This man felt there was more doctrine in Romans than any other letter by Paul, so he put Romans first. (This is the man who gave us the beginnings of the Protestant mindset. Note that he was interested in doctrine, teachings, and stringing verses together. It was a doctrine mindset void of any interest in, or need of knowing, *the story*.)

Luther then decided that I Corinthians had the second most doctrines etc. He saw Philemon as having no doctrine in it, so he put that book dead last in all Paul's thirteen letters.

51

Do you see what this man did to us? Remember, he is the father of the Protestant mind!

No one has ever questioned the arrangement Luther made when he produced the first Protestant New Testament. We come to Paul's writings exactly as this man did, to extract doctrine, to create doctrine, to prove doctrine, to prove doctrinal error, and to bend other Christians to our own little doctrinal world.

The story of the first century still remains unknown.

No one has stood up and said, "Learn the story first!" We come to the New Testament entirely as a book of rules or as a glob of pieces of a jigsaw puzzle to be studied, arranged and then gathered up from all over Scripture, put in categories. And then, poof! You have teachings which tell you what God is like.

And we call this Bible study!? We call this "knowing the Word of God?"*

We need a revolution in Bible study which begins first by recognizing the entire story of the first-century church from beginning to end. (We will not end up having a large number of teachings.) We will be humbled. Many of our idols will fall. We will change, or we will know that we live in a Christian world that is not biblical but a world built

---

*Worst of all, some Christians come to Scripture almost as a ouija board that tells them what to do. "Close your eyes. Open the Bible. Point. Poke. Eureka! There at the end of your finger is the mind of God."

on ideas of our own. . .which we conveniently find *in verses*!

(To wit: No man has ever even attempted to justify the modern-day pastor by means of *the story*. The modern pastor can only be justified if you gather up verses from all over the Bible and make incredible leaps of logic and wild interpretations. Nothing even remotely similar to the modern pastor existed in the first century. Why not use the story? Because the present-day practice of the pastor *never* appears in the first-century story. Disjointed verses taken out of context, then woven together and explained by interpretations, is our *only* justification for the existence of that which is the present-day practice of the pastoral role.)

No one seems to know the story, but if we ever do see it, then the story can never be subservient to a pile of scattered verses. The verses must yield to the story! The disjointed, categorized, systemized verses must give way, *first*, to the story.

Let us learn the story. All of it. From beginning to end, in chronological order.

I trust you can see the slight possibility that there is a little room to consider starting all over again, in a whole new way.

But in so doing, you must also see some practices so deeply embedded in us that most of us are hardly aware of them.

For instance. . .

4

Deep Dependence, Even Psychological Dependence, On the Clergy

A deep dependency on the clergy? This is a subconscious thing yet very real, very powerful, affecting us profoundly. How deep? How real? How much does it grip us and limit us? How detrimental is it to the kingdom of God? And do not men in the clergy unconsciously work from the viewpoint that the clergy is central rather than the saints being central?

Come with me to a Bible study class meeting in some living room. Just ordinary folks are there. No minister has ever been present. (Everyone present in the room is a layman. Everyone works for a living and no one is a professional minister. And those meeting are having lots of fun and joy, freedom and peace.)

Tonight, for the first time, a pastor comes and visits the meeting. Does his presence change the chemistry of that meeting? Yes. Absolutely. You *will* act differently in the presence of a minister. One way or another, you will be affected by a minister's presence.

A small illustration. Here is an illustration which is much more telling.

Let us consider the house church movement. The house church movement is, generally speaking, the most radical thing around these days.

You come into the living room and sit down. The man you see who is leading this particular house church meeting has started a total of *ten* home churches. He is in charge. His people love him. But join him for breakfast some morning at a cafe. Listen to his words. He will tell you what God showed *him*, how *he* began, how the Lord taught *him* things along the way, problems *he* has faced, solutions God gave *him*. He may talk for hours and never mention *you*. Yes, *you*, the layman. In his heart, in his mind, in the very molecular structure of his being, he is the center of this work. For sure, the laymen in those house churches are not the center.

Dare we say the laymen he leads are but a means to achieve his goal. Instruments of *his* ministry.

His battle is not for the layman to emerge free of any need of him. Consciously or unconsciously his battle is for these house churches to remain intent on keeping him their leader.

Go, also, to a para-church organization or to a missionary in the church he raised up in some foreign land. So, also, of course, the traditional church. Perhaps the one sentence which best reveals this malady of clergy dependence and clergy centeredness is, "We must return to giving the laymen more responsibility in the church."

That sentence seems to give hope, does it not? Well, as long as we can even think that sentence, there is no hope for revolution in Christendom.

Look at the words, "*We* must *let* laymen. . ." "*We* must *give* the laymen. . ." Do you not realize that there is still someone in charge, *giving* and *letting*. Not *all* laymen in charge of all things. No, a particular leader, *letting*.

For us to ever see the day that laymen are in charge (with no "letting") means starting over at the beginning. It is the *only* way. Clergyism is too ingrained in the present way of doing things.

Dare you start anew, then it must be in such a way that, *from the beginning*, it is understood that the direction and leadership of the church will soon fall totally in the hands of all the local brothers and sisters. Soon. . .a day when no clergy is in sight. So, also, no elders. No deacons. So, also, no *one* local person leading.

If you have anyone local who is leader; if you have *leaders*; if you have leaders who stay or if you have an individual who later becomes the leader— if you have any of these forces at work in the ekklesia at its *birth* and in its *early stages* of development— there will be no revolution.

No, we must move far beyond such worn-out ways.

It is virtually impossible for the present Protestant mind to conceive of such a church, a church which is left alone by a church planter and, at the time of his leaving, there being no specific leaders.

Many will tell you this is wishful thinking and that it is impossible.

Well, it is happening, right now, here on this planet.

For a moment see in your mind a group of Christians. Let us say they are twenty-five in number. An outsider started them. He just left. He will not be back for a year or two. Where is the clergy? Where is the elder? Where is the local leader? *There is no such person.* Impossible?

Well, dear reader, that is a scene plucked right out of the first century. *That is the way things are supposed to be!*

What on earth do these leaderless folks do? Panic? Call a pastor? Select elders?

If the church planter has raised up that body of believers first-century style, they will know exactly what to do.

Drop the entire Western organizational mind. That is all we have ever seen. What's left? Not much. Try to see a *Christian* version of tribal! (That is not it, but we are struggling here to grasp new and radical dimensions.)

Just what would that be?

Her name is *Ekklesia!*

If these believers have been raised up correctly by the church planter, they will, at this point, revert to primitive *ekklesia*. Yes, they will hold together until the organic nature of the church begins to emerge.

Try explaining this and someone will go out tomorrow and try to do it, and then come back a little later and say it can't be done. You have to see it. You have to be in it. You have to experience it. Even then, you still cannot explain it.

No, it is not explainable. This version of ekklesia can only be *experienced.* You experience church life *first.* After that you give up trying to explain it. You also thank God you did not go out and try to start such a radical version of church life without having first experienced it.

Here is one thing you *cannot do* without first experiencing it.

What happens to these twenty-five people? Those saints, bereft of their outside leader and bereft of any leadership from *within*, grab hold of one another and hold on for dear life. This moment of being left all alone is a moment of joy, excitement, adventure, discovery, and sheer terror!

Eventually, out of the Lord's good mercies, emerges the most vital, vibrant, capable and creative force on this earth. Ekklesia! And through it all they are *never* dependent on the clergy. Not ever.

Sound great? Or does it sound strange? Most of all, is this possible? Does such a version of "church" have any scriptural grounds? Did they do things like this in the first century? Yes, in fact, the church coming into reality in this way is a large part of the first century *story*.

Laymen directing the church? Fear and dependency and awe of ministers replaced by blue collar and white collar laymen, and laymen being all that the church is? A clergyless, lay-everything?

How can that be? How did they make this happen in Century One?

5

Suicidal Church Planting

If you are a layman, the following may be the most life-altering chapter you will ever read.

THE WAY CHURCHES WERE PLANTED

Ladies and gentlemen, behold the *first century's* way of planting churches. Or behold: a study in the suicidal ways of God. . .first-century style. As you read, see if this is something you are familiar with. (The following really is in Scripture!)

To see how each of the churches were raised up, first-century style, we must rediscover the itinerant church planter. That particular type of man exists to plant a church. His *way*: to plant one church in a city and then get out! He departs the church he planted in such a way that he can leave the *entire* church in the hands of the *entire* church! The entire church is left, and it is left to sink or swim. Is this really true? Did it actually happen this way? Better the question be asked: How did we ever get the idea that it was supposed to happen any other way? Is there anything else besides this in Scripture?

The Story

Here is the opening scene. Paul and Barnabas are leaving Antioch and going to the island of Cyprus. From there they go to the regions of Galatia. After two years these two church planters leave Galatia and in so doing, *leave* four new churches.

The next major scene opens with Paul and Silas again leaving Antioch, this time going to Greece to plant churches.

The last major scene opens with Paul going to plant a church in Ephesus.

We are about to look at something unbelievably radical, yet it is as plain to see as a French nose! Even though it is so clear in Scripture, I have money in my clothes which says *no one* has ever preached on the following subject. (If he actually did, and then attempted to live up to what he preached, he probably lost his job as a minister!)

The passages you are about to look at serve to illustrate how we can read the New Testament and not see the obvious. (It also shows how churches are supposed to be planted.)

Let's now go back over those three church planting journeys.

Here is the way things were, in Century One. (The scenes will unfold *chronologically.*)

In Paul's first two journeys there were eight churches raised up. Paul left all of them early on. All departures were in about four short months after the church was born. There was one exception. In five of these churches, Paul was forced out of town. In *two* cases, he left voluntarily. At Corinth he stayed eighteen months.*

The First Church Planting Journey

Two men are sent out by the Holy Spirit to plant churches (not to win souls, mind you, but to plant churches) among the Gentiles. These two men are Paul and Barnabas. Look at what these two men do. Here is the record. The focus is on the word in italics.

> The two men *leave* Antioch, Syria
> and go to Cyprus.
>
> Acts 13:4

> Paul and Barnabas stay just one
> month on Cyprus and *leave.*
>
> Acts 13:13

> The two men go to a city in Pisidia,
> Galatia. (A city where no one has
> ever heard the name Jesus Christ.)

See any chronological outline of this period of time.

They plant a church in this town and after four months, they *leave* the church in Antioch in Pisidia, totally abandoning this new, young, fragile church. Mind you, at the end of four months, they *leave!*

Acts 13:14, 50

Next, Paul and Barnabas go to a town called Iconium. Among the ex-heathen there the gospel is preached. A church is planted in Iconium. In about five months. . .the two church planters *leave.*

Acts 13:51-14:6

The two men, having *left* a young church in Iconium, now walk to a town called Lystra and plant a church there. After about four months in Lystra, the two church planters forsake that new church, *leaving* all things in local hands, with not a designated leader in sight anywhere.

Acts 14:20

The two church planters, having *left* Lystra, go to a small town called Derbe. There they once again raise

up a church. A short time later the
two church planters *leave* Derby!

Acts 14:21

(Note that all these churches found their
leadership not in clergy but in the hands of all the
believers. Paul and Barnabas and the Holy Spirit
pick elders from among *all* the men. See Acts 14:
24)

The two church planters *leave* the
whole area. Paul and Barnabas *leave*
all four new churches. These
churches are hundreds of miles from
the other churches in Syria. The two
men do not only leave, but they *do
not return* again to these four frail
gatherings for *two* long years!
Think about it: In just two years
there were four churches raised up.
No more than four or five months of
help was given each church. The
scene closes with the two men leaving
Galatia and returning home to
Antioch, Syria. . .*leaving* the four
churches all alone.

Acts 14:24 - 26

It is the only way to experience church planting.
May *you* have this joyful, wild, adventurous
experience.

This is New Testament.

This is but the beginning of the near insanity of first-century church planting. . .raising up churches and leaving them.

The Second Church Planting Journey

Paul, now with Silas, once more *leaves* Antioch, Syria to visit those four churches he had deserted two years earlier. Surely Paul will stay longer with the four churches this time.

No, Paul stays in Galatia only a few weeks. He *leaves* them *again* after just a few days with each church! (When Paul *left* Galatia he went to a country called Greece, to plant four more churches.)

> Remember, after a few days Paul ups and *leaves* the four churches in Galatia. The second time! He even *takes from* these churches the one person in all these churches who has shown the most sign of outstanding leadership.
>
> Acts 15:40 - 16:6

> Then Paul makes a *brief* visit to the church in Troas and *leaves* it.
>
> Acts 16:8 - 11

> Paul goes to Greece. He arrives in a town called Philippi. He raises up a church in Philippi. After a few tumultuous days, Paul *leaves*!
>
> Acts 16:40

Paul goes to Thessalonica, plants a church there and very soon (no more than three months) he *departs* the church in Thessalonica.

Acts 17:1, 17:10

Paul arrives in Berea, plants a church in Berea and then *leaves* after only a few weeks.

Acts 17:10, 17:14

Paul then goes to a city in the south of Greece called Corinth and there raises up a church. The Lord has to tell Paul *not* to leave Corinth. Paul stays eighteen months and then he *leaves*.

Acts 17:18

Paul *leaves* all four of these new churches he raised up in Greece. Four churches: Philippi, Thessalonica, Berea, Corinth left. Three were left after about four months; one was left when the church was eighteen months old. He leaves them and goes home to Antioch for another *two* years! (Actually, he leaves *eight* churches in all. Those first four churches he raised up in Galatia are not getting any more help from him either, except a short visit at the beginning of this second trip. That is all the four churches in Galatia get from Paul in six years!

Add it up. Those first four churches in *six years*—have each had about *five months* of help.

Acts 18:21

Now see Paul leave Antioch to go out on a third *church planting* expedition. After staying in Antioch, Syria for a time, Paul sets out for Galatia, making another quick visit to the four churches there.

Count the times each of these four Galatian churches have had Paul, their church planter, present: (1) four months. (2) A week. (3) Another week. Add all this up. It now comes out to about five months of help in *eight* years.

After this last short hello, Paul *leaves* Galatia again!

Acts 18:23

Can any minister on this earth make such a claim? Less than six months of "professional" ministry after raising up a church—leaving it, and spending a total of maybe six months with them in six years.

Oh, Paul, may your tribe increase!

Dear God, may you give us back the ekklesia

who finds her direction in no one except the brothers and sisters of the church— and whose birth and history are intertwined with a man who never stays long. (See also the next chapter.)

The Third Journey

A church planter plants. Except for visits from time to time, all else is left to the local saints. The church planter comes back to a church, *infrequently*. The church planter *is* needed. The local brothers leading when he is not there is *also* needed. Both ingredients are needed. Both, *not* one! Not one and not the other, but both.

This insane way of raising up churches continues: It is the first-century story!

Now let us watch the time line of Paul's third church planting journey. . .

> Paul leaves Galatia and arrives in Ephesus to plant a church. He stays in Ephesus about three years.
> During his second year in Ephesus he goes out into the area surrounding Ephesus planting churches. He has eight men with him whom he is training. There in the small towns near Ephesus, the eight men watch Paul plant churches.
>
> Acts 19:1
>
> At the end of about three years, Paul *leaves* Ephesus and the entire

province of Asia Minor, in order to go to Jerusalem and to return home to Antioch. Whether or not he ever saw his home church again, we do not know. He briefly visits the Greek churches on his way back home to Antioch. Never again will most of these ten or twelve churches even see his face!

Acts 19:21, 20:1, 2

One place where Paul stays on his way to Jerusalem is Corinth. He stays for three months.

Acts 20:3

Add it up. Here is *The Grand Total:*

In eleven years of church planting Paul has made over twenty-five departures. He leaves *twenty-five* times. He has left nine* churches he raised up. In eleven years! (The modern minister boasts of how many years he has stayed in one place. Paul's boast would be in how short a time he stayed.)

Further, the average time spent with most of these churches—stretched out over a period of eleven years—is still about six months. The exceptions? Corinth: eighteen months plus two later

Nine which we know by name during the three church planting journeys.

**You might want to read these other references to Paul's leaving churches. (I Cor 16:3-9; II Cor. 12:14)*

visits. . .one month and three months. Total, twenty-two months. Ephesus: about three-and-a-half years. All the others: six months in eleven years.**

Paul's total time of ministry from the day he and Barnabas departed Antioch until he was arrested and placed in jail in Jerusalem was about *eleven* years. The total of Paul's entire ministry of planting churches was no more than fifteen years!

Repeat: Paul had an active ministry as a church planter of only about fifteen years. If you and I return to this way of *ekklesia* life, it really will be a *lay* church. That way of planting churches, that way of churches being abandoned, that way of the local believers being responsible for *everything*—and clergyless while doing so—*that* is *beyond* radical!

You have seen the *one* revolutionary ingredient which was in the first century. It is the church planter coming into a city, planting a church, staying a short period and leaving the new church on its own for a long period.

This, dear reader, is *beyond* the most *radical* things happening in our day. Let us hope we see such church planters on this earth again: men who plant and leave.

That brings us to the other revolutionary ingredient. It, too, is *beyond radical.* What is it?

Needed: men who plant and leave. *And* men and women willing to be an ekklesia when the church planter departs. . .saints who are willing to be left alone and willing to launch out on the greatest adventure of all: discovering ekklesia. . .all on their own!

This next chapter may reveal more clearly this other life-changing idea, one more radical than you are *ever* exposed to.

6

One Very Earth-Shaking Word

Paul left every church he ever raised up (on those first two church planting trips of his), and left them without any leaders. No leaders of any sort. What did those folks, abandoned by their church planter, do?

No one seems to have noticed, but the Scripture tells us, plainly, what they did in the first century.

What you are about to read is a thought new to Christians in our day. Seventeen hundred years have passed since men thought, acted and experienced the way the early followers of Christ did.

You are about to see unfold the most radical way ecclesiology can be looked upon. (Please note that we are going through the New Testament chronologically, the *entire story* in context. I have money in my clothes no one in his right mind has ever stood up in a church and spoken on this obvious subject. He would be advocating that the clergy

leave, and the church move into community. . .
without leaders.)

The power of desperate men and women, left
alone, is breathtaking and beautiful.

See these first-century believers, without
education, illiterate, and poor beyond our ability to
imagine. Still those people and those churches
survived. Survived and then *flourished*. Flourished
and then scared the life out of the civilization of
that day.

All we are going to do right now is look at one
word. One terribly overlooked word. One very
powerful word. That word is:

brothers!

What happens when a people—that is, an
ekklesia—are forsaken by their church planter?
Here are the ingredients of high adventure: (1)
church planters who leave, and (2) brothers and
sisters who uniquely, valiantly, creatively, daringly
. . .allow themselves to be left all alone!

(You might ask some of them. Such people *do*
exist today!)

As we look at the incredible record left to us in
Scripture, let the reality of the experience of the
first-century ekklesia come alive before your eyes.

Pause and ask yourself: "Have I ever been part
of any church where not only the word *brother* but
the *action* of brothers and sisters so filled the church
life?"

Have you ever heard of a church so much in the hands of, not a minister, not elders, not one local leader, but in the hands of an entire gathering utterly centered on the *corporate deeds of the men and women of the church.*

Have you ever considered or even dreamed of such a church?

We look first in Acts as we behold these amazing men who were left, abandoned men, who so often watched their church planter leave.

ACTS

Peter stood up in front of 120 people and began, "Brothers and sisters. . ."

1:15, 16

It was from *the brothers* that seven men were chosen.

6:3

Note that it was the action of the *brothers and sisters* in the church, not leaders of any sort, who got Paul out of town, fast.

9:30

Peter left Joppa to go to another town. Some of the *brothers* in the church in Joppa accompanied him. (Your church does this all the time, doesn't it?)

10:23

The apostles and the *brothers* heard.*

11:1

Peter struggles with whether or not
to go visit Gentiles. Six *brothers* go
with him. (Apostles and brothers—
these are the two kinds of people who
occupy the center of the first-century
stage.)

11:12

Brothers in Antioch send relief to the
brothers in Jerusalem.

11:29

Peter, just freed from prison, says,
"Tell James and the *brothers* the
news."

12:17

Paul and Barnabas have a fight with
some Jerusalem believers who have
come to Antioch brandishing a
circumcision knife. Who settled the
issue of what to do with this problem?
Elders? Bishops? No. The *brothers*

*Luke makes an unconscious reference here, revealing his
inate acceptance, to a matrix full of the actions of brothers
and sisters. He is not aware of what he is disclosing to us!
From his unconscious view of things Luke reveals that it is
"Apostles and brothers" who get things done. Not apostles,
elders and deacons.

did. But those brothers (and sisters) could not possibly have handled such an issue unless, for a long time before, they had led and guided the ekklesia in Antioch. The men in the church in Antioch were joined at the hip. . . working together. . . from the beginning of the existence of the church in Antioch.

15:1, 2

The church in Jerusalem was now sixteen years old. It now had *elders*. Sixteen years, mind you. Those elders were just plain brothers long before they became elders. May it ever be. A church around ten years old is a nice number to have elders, elders in the age we live in when men know nothing of just plain brothers being fully in charge of the ekklesia *before* any gifts or offices emerge. (Especially is this true because men of our age are so "title happy.")

It was the *brothers* in the churches in Antioch who decided to send Paul and Barnabas to Jerusalem to face apostles and elders. Yes, but the *brothers* also sent a few of the *brothers* among themselves along with them.

15:2

As Paul and Barnabas headed south toward Jerusalem, they stopped in the churches in Phoenicia as well as those in Samaria. They told the churches about heathen Gentiles being converted. The *brothers* in those churches rejoiced with great joy.

15:3

The entire church in Jerusalem—even though it had elders—picked out some of the *brothers* to go tell the church in Antioch of the results of the Jerusalem conference. The church in Jerusalem did not send elders to the church in Antioch. It sent *brothers*. Two men who were *leaders* among the brothers, but men not carrying any title, were picked by all the brothers and sisters.

15:12

The apostles and elders in Jerusalem sent a letter to Antioch. The letter is signed by apostles and leaders but it is received in Antioch by *brothers*. In fact, the letter is addressed *to brothers*. . .not leaders. (Probably there were none.)

Just what kind of amazing relationship did men in Antioch have with one another that the men in Jerusalem would send a letter to the *brothers*?

15:23

To whom do Silas and Judas speak when they arrive in Antioch? To the *brothers*. It was a term that poured out of the mouths and out of the pen because of the way things were. Ministers were not in charge; today's idea of clergy did not exist. Nor did today's concept of elders exist, either.

15:33

(Of course, the present-day church does such things all the time, doesn't it?)

Paul and Barnabas decide to go back to Galatia to visit the four churches they had planted there in Galatia four years earlier. In describing their plans, they say unconsciously (because this is the way things were): "Let's go visit the *brothers*." Paul's mind was to go see his brothers in Galatia. Not elders or ministers— just his dear brothers up there in Galatia.

15:36

(Your church, based on its daily experience and its daily actions and its very matrix, talks about "the brothers doing this and that" and "visiting the brothers in the other churches" all the time, does it not?)

You are seeing in this word *brothers* the natural vocabulary of a church. The simple reason for these reoccurring references is that all the brothers in a church were *in charge of the church!* Not a minister. Not elders.

Paul and Barnabas now have a falling out. They split up. Barnabas goes to Cyprus. Silas goes with Paul.

> The *brothers* in the church in Antioch gather around Paul and Silas and send them on their way. (The church of our day does this all the time, doesn't it?)
>
> 15:40

Can you see the fluidity of the brothers in the churches and the responsibility they shoulder. . . daily? We now pause in the book of Acts at the point where Paul writes his first epistle. This brings us to a place in Acts where Paul writes a letter. Let us look at his words. Again, we take this letter in chronological order.

Paul's Letters Reveal *Brothers*

It is at this point (Acts 15:40) that Paul, still in

80

Antioch but getting ready to go to Galatia, writes a letter to the four Galatian churches. Why? Because those knife-wielding, circumcision-happy Jews from Jerusalem have gone to those four churches up in Galatia for the purpose of changing all those Gentiles into Mosaic Jews. Turning Paul's ex-heathen converts into Jews! Consequently, the four churches are in a crisis—a crisis worse than you have ever been in. But as Paul picks up his pen to write these four churches, does he make even one reference to elders? Or professional ministers?

Galatians—Paul's first letter

Paul opens his letter to the four Gentile churches by saying to them that all the *brothers and sisters* in Antioch send their greetings. Then, seven times in his letter to the Galatians, Paul implores, begs and pleads with the *brothers and sisters*. Not once does he refer to leaders. No reference to elders in this entire letter. . .only references to those who run the church: the *brothers and sisters*. It is to *brothers*, not elders, that church planters turn when the church is in crisis.

It was the brothers and sisters leading each of those four churches in Galatia. Nobody else.

This is *revolutionary* ecclesiology, folks.

Let's now return to Acts. The writer of Acts tells us that Paul returned to Galatians (after he wrote his letter to them).

81

Paul arrives back in Galatia. In each town he sits down with the *brothers and sisters* in the churches. In the church in Lystra and in the church in Derbe the *brothers and sisters* there tell Paul about the amazing young Timothy.

Acts 16:2

Paul and Silas move on to Greece. They get beaten and thrown in jail in the town of Philippi. They have been in that city for no more than one to three months. But *brotherhood* has taken root among the brothers in the ekklesia there. The two church planters depart Philippi with the church void of all leadership except the *brothers and the sisters*.

Acts 16:40

A mob in the town of Thessalonica could not find Paul so they beat some of the *brothers* in the ekklesia.

Acts 17:6

Thessalonians

The church in Thessalonica is three months old. The church is under persecution from the townspeople and government. Paul's life is in danger. On top of that the Thessalonian Christians are about to be left utterly alone and leaderless. They have only known the Lord three months; nonetheless, the men in the church have become brothers to one another. (Brotherhood and sisterhood, dear reader, is powerful stuff!) These *brothers and sisters*—and no one else—are in charge of things. In the midst of this crisis the *brothers* encircled Paul. They decided to wait until night and at that time sneak Paul out of town. Action: by an already-formed brotherhood, in a very young church.

> A "brother and sister" approach is already born in Thessalonica! All in three months. A three-month old church in a heathen land, under persecution, is in the hands of local leadership—which is simply all the brothers in the church.
>
> Acts 17:10
>
> (Your church can do this, can't it? And the men in the church are in charge, right?)

When you come to Acts 18:5 you find that Paul has made his way to Corinth. While there, he receives a letter from the Christians up in Thessalonica. Paul answers their letter. In his letter to the brothers and sisters in Thessalonica, Paul addresses the brothers and sisters *fourteen* times. Fourteen times in one letter!

Some in the church in Thessalonica misinterpret some of Paul's words. Chaos ensues. The church in Thessalonica is in a new crisis. This crisis is internal. Paul writes a second letter to the church, including one sentence in which he adjures *every brother and sister* in the church to hear this letter read.

There is no reference in all that letter to clergy or elders, even though the church is in a royal mess. In this second letter to this young and crises-ridden church, Paul directly addresses the *brothers and sisters six* times. And *none* to clergy or elders.

We return again to Acts as we move along chronologically. Paul is leaving Corinth.

> When Paul departed from Corinth he had been there eighteen months, long enough to have appointed elders. But he did not. When he left the church in Corinth, the brothers and sisters in Corinth, welded together, were in charge.
>
> Acts 18:18

Now look at Acts 18 and see just how clearly is the reality of the church's brotherhood being in charge of the ekklesia.

> The *brothers and sisters* in one church wrote a letter to the *brothers and sisters* in another church.
>
> Acts 18:27

(You belong to a church where it is the brothers in the church—not pastors nor elders—who decide to write letters to other churches, then compose and send the letters. . .don't you?)

At least six years pass before Paul pens another letter. By that time Paul is in Ephesus. The letter he next writes is to the church in Corinth. The church in Corinth is nearly eight years old, and the church is in a very serious crisis. This crisis provoked two letters from Paul to the Corinthians. See just how revealing is Paul's inbred point of reference.

Corinthians

Paul writes the church in Corinth *two* letters. Remember, this is the worst internal church crisis recorded in the New Testament. (The letters were written in the period reported on in Acts 19.)

In his *first* letter to Corinth, Paul addresses, advises, exhorts, implores the *brothers and sisters* in the church 24 times. He never refers to the existence of any other kind of leaders. Again, there are only two kinds of people on the stage of first-century Christianity: (1) church planters and (2) brothers and sisters.

Think how revolutionary this is to our present-day outlook.

Even a cursory reading of these passages leaves no doubt who is in charge locally. It is not clergymen, nor elders. . .but rather it is *all the brethren* in the church.

In Paul's *second* letter to Corinth he addresses the local brothers in the church *four* more times! But, surprisingly, he makes mention of brothers in other churches, who are taking action in *their* churches, and of sending a brother here and a brother there, *four* times.

(Eight references in all in II Corinthians.)

We are still looking at all these events in *chronological* order. We make our way through Acts until we come to the place in Acts where Paul writes a letter to a church in Italy! See Acts 20:4, which refers to the point in time where Paul wrote to the Romans.

Romans

Paul, leaving Ephesus, visited the ekklesia in Corinth. While there he sat down and wrote a letter to the Christians in Rome. Most of these in Rome who receive Paul's letter were personal friends of Paul. In fact, Paul actually sent many of these people to Rome. (Once more, two factors at work in the first century . . . church planters, and the brothers and sisters.) He picked believers out of the churches in Asia Minor, Galatia, Syria and Israel and sent them—working together—to raise up a Gentile church in Rome.

86

Despite the fact this book to the Romans is essentially a doctrinal treatise, from Chapter One through Eleven, Paul directly addresses *the brothers and sisters* in the church in Rome *nine* times.

There are no references to clergy or elders in Rome.

Paul, who was in Ephesus, started home, to Antioch. He was ending his third *church planting* trip. Arriving at Ptolemais he greeted the brothers and sisters* in the church in Ptolemais and spent the night there.

Do you get a group sense—that untitled men and women lead the ekklesia?

Paul finally returned back to Antioch, then went to Jerusalem where he was warmly received by the brothers and sisters. Shortly after arriving there, he was arrested and eventually sent to Rome.

Paul's Arrival in Italy

There is so much pathos in Acts 28:14 - 15. Paul has been in prison for two years and has gone through a horrendous shipwreck (his fourth). Paul, the prisoner, finally reached Italy and began making his journey to Rome. *Brothers* in Rome heard he was on his way to Rome. They came out to meet him.

And so he took courage, and so he came to Rome—Acts 28:16.

So ends Acts.

---

*Acts 21:7

But the end of Acts does not mean the end of Paul's letters to churches. Until now we have stayed with *the story*, chronologically.

We now continue to do so even though, chronologically, the book of Acts has come to an end. The story goes on far *beyond* Acts.

Colossians and Ephesians

While in Rome as a prisoner, Paul writes two letters to the churches in Colossae, Heiropolis, and Laodicea. These are cities he has never visited, churches he did not raise up and has never seen.

These three churches were raised up by a man named Epaphroditus. Epaphroditus left Colossae. When Paul wrote to the church in Ephesus, Epaphroditus was in Italy.

Church planters *depart!*

Remember, Paul writes those two brief letters to churches which have *no* leaders, nor do they have their church planter. Paul has never met these people, nonetheless, it is obvious that these churches are led not by anyone except the *brothers and sisters*. In three different places he speaks to those whom he has never met, referring to them as "brethren." He never addressed anyone else! Just *brothers and sisters* and *saints*.

Philippians

About six months after writing to Colossae, Paul writes his *last* letter to a church. In the nine letters

Paul writes to churches, it is *only* here that he makes his one reference to elders.

But keep this in mind: This church he is writing to is 12 years old! And remember, those elders were brothers in the church and brothers in brothers gatherings—just plain brothers—*long* before they were ever elders. Probably, if those elders tried to pull off some "submission and authority" bondage, the brothers in that church would remind their high-flying elders that they, like everyone else, are just ordinary men.

With *one* reference to elders in this short letter to the Philippians, there are *six* places where Paul implores the *brothers* to take action in certain matters. Not elders! The brothers and sisters still appear to be very much in charge.

In nine letters Paul wrote to churches, he made only one reference to elders. In this one short letter he made *six* references to the brethren. Paul made scores of references directly addressed to the brothers in each locale. And it is to the only church not under siege that he mentions elders!

How many churches can you name which live in this matrix?

God give us men—*church planters*—who make things happen in this way. Give us *departing*, leaving, travelling church planters. *And* give us brothers and sisters who are willing to be utterly abandoned by the church planter and who then grasp their paddles and paddle like crazy!

You have now seen the second ingredient necessary to raising up churches in the first century. The first is church planters—church planters who leave. Second, you see the church led only by, solely by, the entire local gathering—nobody else.

(Isn't it amazing. Hundreds of thousands of books have been written about ministers. Air castles, worlds, whole realms have been created by these books, centralizing everything on the minister and romanticizing the pastor, priest, etc. But no one ever wrote a book based just on *these* passages, presenting the *real* saga, that of ordinary men and women and what they did. Where is *one* lone book on *brothers*?)

Men and women, left alone, experiencing and discovering church life. And church planters who are rarely around.

Truly, this is *beyond radical*.

Do you think you would like to see such men roaming the earth again? Yes? Well, how do you feel about your being caught up in such a "brothers and sisters" drama? You think maybe you are willing to be abandoned by all outside leadership, thrown with a bunch of brothers and sisters in what could turn out to be a leaky boat?

If the answer is *yes*, then it is possible you are ready to move beyond radical. Let the point be made: The churches of Century One *were* begun by itinerant church planters and led by laymen.

Will we ever see church planters of this strip again?

7

Church Planter, Where Are You?

We need church planters of the first century breed. And we need such brothers and sisters as those in Century One, who took all responsibility for all the church's commission and ran with it. Two very big needs. There is no doubt that if we had such church planters, there would then be plenty of such brothers and sisters, and paddles to row with. Why are there not such church planters around? There are good reasons.

The first reason: (And no one seems willing to do this) All church planters should first grow up in real, honest-to-goodness, non-theoretical, living, breathing, free-swinging, freedom-filled, legalistic-free, law-free, *church life*. Growing up in church life *before* ever daring to plant a church.

Live in the church as an ordinary brother. That comes *first!* Most ministers will not stop, lay down their tradition-ridden ministry, and do this. Most ministers have two or three subconscious ideas about the ministry.

One: "I've got to go save the world from hell; I can't stop for two or three years and be a layman!"

Second: "Me, get a job? Are you crazy? I'll starve!"

Third: "I've just had a revelation. I now see all these things. . . therefore, I can do without having to stop my ministry! I'm going out to plant churches."

Answers:

One: No, you do not.

Two: It's good for you.

Three: You can't.

Concerning number three: You underestimate the job and overestimate your ability. Sit for a few years and let clergy flow out of you. (It does that very thing when you work for a living.)

Discover church life. You will then get on your knees and thank God you did *not* try to go out and plant churches before you experienced church life.

A little humility, a time resting, a time of learning in the best of all seminaries: the ekklesia.

A time to learn to experience Jesus Christ never hurt a clergyman. Yet church life, (real, organic church life,) continues to be a thing too radical to grasp for most men called of God. Much less attempting to plant one when you have never even been in one. But you will learn that fact *only* when you are in church life. . .as an ordinary person.

Paradoxically, the more radical such men are, the more gifted they are, the less likely they are willing to sit.

When, then, are men called of God willing to move *beyond radical*?

It seems every generation produces only one or two such fool-hardy men. Beyond that, I know of no explanation why, out of five, ten or twenty million ministers per century, *none* take this route. . .a route so obviously the way things were done in the first century. It may boil down to a matter of humility, of brokenness, of desperation, of revelation, or of the capacity to *risk*. It may simply be the lack of "being poor in spirit." Surely it is not money, is it? Or loss of acceptance?

Perhaps you are wondering if it is scriptural to first experience church life *before* being a minister.

Let's see.

8

Before Churches Are Raised Up

Church planters first grew up in church life! They grew up in those churches so oddly planted. They did so before they become church planters! Is that really in Scripture? Yes!

● The first twelve church planters experienced an embryonic church life while living with Jesus Christ for four years. This was what those men—called of God—did before they raised up the church in Jerusalem.

● Barnabas, Agabus, Stephen, Philip, Silas, Justus all experienced church life before becoming workers.

When these men went out, please note that the churches stood behind them, utterly. Why? Because the church knew these men at close range and were eager to help them, and because they were trustworthy men, proven in the daily living of church life. The other brothers in the church really knew these men. . .and loved them and backed them anyway. I would say a church that is experiencing true church life will back any man in their midst who is called of God—who has first lived among them—unless they feel he is some kind of nut or unless they feel the time is premature for him. Or unless he is simply not the material for the job. Saints in the singularity of church life love to help such men. (No, not the nuts, the other kind.)

● Paul sat under Barnabas four years in the church in Antioch before setting out on his first church planting journey. The church in Antioch stood behind Paul when he went out.

● Later, in Ephesus, Paul trained eight *Gentile* church planters just as Jesus had trained twelve Jewish church planters. The way Paul did this was pure genius. Paul chose gentlemen who had all lived in Gentile churches.

The only trainers of workers were church planters. Those almost planters, themselves, first lived in church life. Remember: They grew up in churches planted by church planters. Departing, leaving. . .church planters.

It was men who had lived in church life whom Paul called to Ephesus for their training. Every one of those men had *previously* been in a local body of believers before going to Ephesus. All eight of these Gentile men had been saved in, and grew spiritually *in*. . .church life. Is this really in Scripture?

Aristarchus and Secundus were saved in and grew up in the church in Thessalonica.

Sopater: The church in Berea.

Gaius: The church in Derbe.

Timothy: The church in Lystra.

Tychicus and Trophemus: The church in Ephesus.

Titus: The church in Antioch.

see Acts 20:4

These are the eight men Paul trained. Later was added to this number Epaphroditus, who appears to have been converted in the church in Ephesus, even though his home town was Colossae. (The town of Colossae was about ninety miles from Ephesus.) He went back to Colossae, Heiropolis, and Laodicea, raised up a church in each of the three towns, and then *left* them!

All these men lived in church life before becoming church planters. All sat under and were trained by a church planter. (*This* ain't seminary, folks.) All these men experienced church life *before!*

Only the worker named *Apollos* did not first experience church life before becoming a worker . . .and Apollos was a pain to everyone!

Now you see at least one reason why we have so few such men and why we need such men so desperately.

Anyone for revolution?*

* *Please see* Overlooked Christianity, *SeedSowers Publishing House. It is about how men were trained in the first century.*

* * *

Dear reader, if you are a minister or a young seminarian who feels called of God, do not lay down your ministry and become an ordinary brother in church life just because it sounds like a good idea, or even because it is scriptural. Do so only by revelation. Teeth-jarring, soul-shaking revelation. Please! Sir, some things are not practices, they are holy revealings come from God to you.

To see all these heavy matters being lived again upon the earth—to see a deeply spiritual church raised up by such odd men as *departing* church planters—calls for all of us to go beyond what today is considered radical.

Let us end here.

Either you are one for revolution or you are not.

If you are, there are books to read, tapes to listen to. . . and, perhaps, a church or two which you should visit, so that you can see, firsthand, that such things can really happen. . . here. . .now. . .on planet earth.

The only cause worth living and dying for is a totally hopeless cause.

Addendum

Addendum

Will Things Change?

Let us say that the book you now hold in your hands was read by every minister, pastor and Christian worker in the English-speaking world. What would be its impact? Would next Sunday change, or would next Sunday look just like last Sunday? And what of next year?

Just knowing the historical information of where we got our present practices (which you read in the first three chapters) does not cause men to change what they are now doing. The present practice of evangelical Christianity is going to go on. Forever. That, dear reader, is just the way things are.

Take the Reformation for an example. Despite the revelation and information which came from that short era of reform, it did not even dent the Roman Catholic Church. The Catholic denomination, with so little Scripture to justify what it does, has nonetheless justified all its practices. . .by means of

Scripture! Evangelical Christianity has as many practices not scriptural, but like the Roman Catholics, it justified its unscriptural non-first-century practice *with* Scripture. You cannot break a deeply engrained mind-set, regardless of facts! Catholicism changed during the reformation not one iota!

Despite this little book, evangelical practices will not change.

Evangelical Christianity has traditions which are buried deep. Those traditions are just as sacred to Protestants and evangelicals as are those the Catholics practice—Scripture or no Scripture.

Things will not change.

There are somewhere between three and five million people in the English-speaking world who make their livelihood by working in today's evangelical churches, organizations, etc.

Imagine the Following

Try to envision pastors giving up their homes and salaries. Imagine missionaries giving up their 300-year-old method of missions and reverting to Paul's way of church planting. Imagine mission boards all over the world closing. . .because, after all, they *are* practicing totally unscriptural ways. Imagine ministers not only leaving the pastorate and parsonage, but getting jobs. . .paying their own way in the ministry by working for a living. Imagine church buildings being abandoned, even boarded up.

Then try to imagine all of God's people willingly returning to home meetings and experiencing *church* without having a minister or having anyone guiding them. . .but, rather, just infrequent visits from their church planter.

Imagine a pastor telling his flock that he will work with them for six more months and then he will leave them so they can carry on by themselves, and that, at the time of his departure, the building will be locked. Everyone will begin meeting in homes, and *he* won't be back to help for two years! And when he does come back, he will only stay two weeks!

Now try to calculate just how many of his members would go along with such a peanut-brain idea! Imagine the elders and deacons willing to lay down their offices and titles. How many ministers do you think would do this? How many parishioners would agree?

Lack of Willingness

And if the first century *story* was known by everyone—instead of no one—how many ministers would stand up and say "Let's return to our well springs!"

Lack of Training

But more, consider this: Are there any ministers who have been trained to raise up a church in so radical a fashion as was carried out in Century One?

Are there any men who have firsthand experience in this odd way of doing things? Or men who have first-hand ever even *seen* it? Men who can prepare the Lord's people for such a wild adventure and such a daring, dangerous transition: Do such men exist? Have any, for a thousand years!

Imagine the seminaries of this world closing and reverting to the ancient concept of the church planter being the trainer of workers. On-the-job training. Imagine evangelical Christianity reverting back to training men the way Jesus and Paul raised up church planters. Imagine *all* ministers being prepared for ministry the way Paul trained up the eight Gentile church planters.

Imagine the dissolving of denominational headquarters! Can you see everyone blithely giving up their jobs to return to the ways found in *the story?*

Without the use of armed force there has never been such a transition. Even when change came by means of the sword, such a radical change as this has *never* been accomplished.

Can you imagine the para-church organizations shutting down? In order to be *scriptural?* The economic stress alone would be horrible. Hundreds of thousands of Christians would be out of a job.

No matter how strongly a man shouts "We must be biblical, scriptural and New Testament, we must obey the Word of God," money, security, hearth and home have a way of rendering sterile that vaunted declaration.

Shall we abandon the man-made practices we have accumulated over the centuries, even if those practices undermine and even destroy our very livelihood?

Shall we rid ourselves of these stumbling blocks, when it would unquestionably throw several million people out of work. . .unemployed. . . penniless? Can you see three or four million Christians who make their living in Christian organizations all quitting. . .and quitting *happily?*

Can you imagine any more than a handful of people being willing to agree to such a scenario even if all 500,000,000 Protestants read this little book?

No, we will not abandon these ways. And Christianity as it is *will* go on as it is.

If you believe (1) these radical changes can occur in today's evangelical churches. . .or (2) that you will work from within those institutions to assist them in making radical change, you are *not* a candidate for revolution.

Please, let these present practices of Protestantism continue. Let them remain in peace. Never attack the status quo. Further, if you are in the present-day practice of Christianity, and you are happy there, *stay* there. Let the traditions and organizations continue.

The only people who belong in a revolution are those who know they simply cannot stay where they are, and that they *must* leave.

When you leave, leave humbly. . .and quietly.

Don't slam the door as you leave. Criticize nothing—the people staying are your brothers and sisters in Christ.

Never be one to drive a knife through an older wineskin, nor to try to place new wine in skin that has lost its ability to stretch.

Jesus lived in the midst of the Jewish religion. He did not seek to end it. Please note this fact! That same religion is *still* here. . .two thousand years later! Jesus wisely said to us to leave things as they are, and let them continue as they are. But he *did* tell us to *leave*.

Be gentle with God's people.

You are, after all, one of God's people, and *you* need *gentle!* Being ugly may belong to radical, but being ugly does not belong in a place *beyond radical!*

You and I will see only part of the revolution. It will come, but it will come slowly. After all, we are considering here a change in the very direction of Christian history—a vast, unprecedented change.

Such a change cannot take place in *one* lifetime. It never has, it never will. Unless, of course, you force the change by the sword! We will not do that.

Recognize the scope, the utter vastness of this revolution. It is a revolution so radical in nature it will take 200 to 300 years to come into full fruition.

Only when Catholics and Protestants can actually look at an experience of the Christian faith that is so beautiful, so simple, so uncluttered, so caring, and can *see* people in it who are so "wowed" by their daily experience of being in church life. . .only then will *some few* drop the old.

Make that at least 300 years

You will probably hear someone say: "Oh, but things will change when persecution comes."

Actually that is not true. Persecution cannot ferret out a mindset. Persecution cannot destroy a religious culture. Please note: The Catholics slaughtered the Lutherans. The Lutherans did not change. The Protestants slaughtered the Catholics. The Catholics did not change. Both drove the other underground; but later, when the persecuted emerged again, they were utterly unchanged in their practices.

Christians from America who visited Russia when it was under communism told of how pure and simple and scriptural the hidden church in Russia was. (How they suffered, how they met in the woods, etc.) Actually, it wasn't all that wonderful. When the Russian underground church re-emerged, it started building church buildings and going back to all the things Protestants do. They reverted—overnight.

Out there in those woods where they had their secret meetings . . .there was still a pastor present. (The pastoral role never ended.) Even there, hiding in the woods, God's people, ever the silent laity, circled around their pastor. There in those woods they sang two songs, prayed, sang two more songs, then prayed again. Then they "passed the plate," and then the pastor spoke. After that came the benediction and they all went back home.

No, persecution will not change the present practice of "church."

They had not changed. When the persecution in Russia ended, the first word to come to the West was, "Please, send us money so that we can build a church building." And today, the Russians still have pastors and a building, and when they meet, they have two songs and. . ."

And the silent laymen. . .sit. And the sitting laymen are silent.

The Centrality of Christ. . .In the Church

Persecution does not change our practice nor our mindset. Only the end of the schematic of our Protestant mindset will bring radical change.

A return to the first-century mind is our only hope. A return to the first-century experience of ekklesia, to the first-century's incredible ability to touch Christ and to intimately know and express Christ. To see Him central. To experience Him as *central* in a church void of clergy, where ownership of the church belongs to all the saints. When daily and weekly direction comes from the brothers and sisters themselves. . .that is our only hope.

That brings us to *you*.

A few questions you need to consider:

Are you so desperate you simply cannot abide the present scenario?

And here is the key question:

Are you willing to become part of a revolution so radical, even *beyond* radical. . .a revolution that cannot possibly succeed in your lifetime? *That* is a revolution, indeed.

The only cause worth living for. . . is a hopeless cause.

This is a hopeless cause.

The persistent call of the voices of radical men and women and the witness of their unprecedented experience. . .*these voices* of believers outside the traditional church . . . stretching out across the centuries. . .this voice alone from saints who have moved *beyond radical*. . .will one day become the greatest influence on Christendom.

That you and I cannot—in one lifetime— possibly win this revolution. . .*that* is what makes this revolution so worthy of our lives.

Would you like to be one of the few people in the last 1800 years who know the story of what happened in Century One? These three books tell that story.

Revolution
The first 17 years

The Silas Diary

The Titus Diary

and coming soon:

The Timothy Diary

You may order
copies of this book from:

SeedSowers Publishing House

P.O. Box 285

Sargent, GA 30275

1-800-228-2665

or in England:

PEER KAPER
99 Trinidad Cres.
Parkstone
Poole
Dorset BH12 3NW

By ordering this book in lots of 50 or more, you may receive them at virtual cost. (With your order you will also receive a catalog listing other books and tapes of similar content!) Let's use this book to launch a revolution.

Radical Books for Radical Christians

If you are interested in house churches, you will want to read the following six books:

Beyond Radical

Revolution

The Silas Diary

The Titus Diary

How to Meet *Under the Headship of Jesus Christ*

An Open Letter to House Church Leaders

When the Church Was Led *Only* **by Laymen**

In addition to these books, there are also over one hundred tapes and videos which are available. You might want to first listen to:

- *Christian, This Is Your Lord!*
- *Making Christ Central*
- *God's Eternal Purpose*

For more information please write:

SeedSowers

P.O. Box 285

Sargent, GA 30275

800-228-2665

Orders of 50 or more of *Beyond Radical* for $3 each. This quantity offer is also good for the booklets *When the Church Was Led Only by Laymen* and *An Open Letter to House Church Leaders for $2 each.*

The SeedSowers

Prices as of 1999.

REVOLUTIONARY BOOKS ON CHURCH LIFE
How to Meet Under the Headship of Jesus Christ (Edwards).....$11.95
An Open Letter to House Church Leaders (Edwards)...................4.00
When the Church Was Led Only by Laymen (Edwards)...............4.00
Beyond Radical (Edwards)..5.95
Rethinking Elders (Edwards)..9.95
Revolution, The Story of the Early Church (Edwards)................8.95
The Silas Diary (Edwards)..9.95
The Titus Diary (Edwards)..TBA
Overlooked Christianity (Edwards)..14.95

AN INTRODUCTION TO THE DEEPER CHRISTIAN LIFE
The Highest Life (Edwards)..8.95
The Secret to the Christian Life (Edwards)..............................8.95
The Inward Journey (Edwards)..8.95

CLASSICS ON THE DEEPER CHRISTIAN LIFE
Experiencing the Depths of Jesus Christ (Guyon)......................8.95
Practicing His Presence (Lawrence)..8.95
The Spiritual Guide (Molinos)..8.95
Song of the Bride (Guyon)..9.95
Union With God (Guyon)..8.95
The Seeking Heart (Fenelon)...9.95
Guyon Speaks Again (Guyon)..14.95
Spiritual Torrents (Guyon)..14.95
The Ultimate Intention (Fromke)..11.00

IN A CLASS BY ITSELF
The Divine Romance (Edwards)..8.95

THE CHRONICLES OF THE DOOR (Edwards)
The Beginning...8.95
The Escape..8.95
The Birth...8.95
The Triumph..8.95
The Return...8.95

THE WORKS OF T. AUSTIN-SPARKS
The Centrality of Jesus Christ..19.95
The House of God...29.95
Ministry..29.95
Service..29.95

COMFORT AND HEALING
A Tale of Three Kings (Edwards)..8.95
The Prisoner in the Third Cell (Edwards)..........................7.95
Letters to a Devastated Christian (Edwards)....................5.95
Crucified by Christians (Edwards).......................................8.95

OTHER BOOKS ON CHURCH LIFE
Climb the Highest Mountain (Edwards)..............................9.95
The Torch of the Testimony (Kennedy)............................14.95
The Passing of the Torch (Chen)..9.95
Going to Church in the First Century (Banks)..................5.95
When the Church was Young (Loosley)............................14.95
The Open Church (Rutz)..8.95
Church Unity (Litzman, Nee, Edwards)...........................14.95
Let's Return to Christian Unity (Kurosaki).....................14.95

CHRISTIAN LIVING
Final Steps in Christian Maturity (Guyon)......................12.95
The Key to Triumphant Living (Taylor)..............................9.95
Turkeys and Eagles (Lord)..8.95
Beholding and Becoming (Coulter)......................................8.95
Life's Ultimate Privilege (Fromke).......................................7.00
Unto Full Stature (Fromke)...7.00
All and Only (Kilpatrick)...7.95

Please write or call for our current catalog:

The SeedSowers
P.O. Box 285
Sargent, GA 30275

800-228-2665

THE ORDER OF PAUL'S LETTERS

Construct your own First-Century Story.

1. Galatians—see Acts 13:12. (It was about here—in Acts' record of events—that Paul wrote to the Galatians.) Written from Antioch, Syria in 49 A.D.

2. I Thessalonians—see Acts 18:1. I Thessalonians was written in late 51 A.D. from Corinth, Greece.

3. II Thessalonians—about 3 months later. See Acts 18:1. Written in early 52 A.D.

4. I Corinthians—six years pass. Written from Ephesus, mid-57 A.D. See Acts 19: 22-23.

5. II Corinthians—written from Ephesus or Philippi in the summer of 57 A.D. See Acts 20:1.

6. Romans—written from Corinth; winter late 57 A.D. or early 58 A.D. See Acts 20:2.

The following letters were written after the close of the book of Acts.

7. Colossians, Ephesians, Philemon—all written from Rome, late 61 A.D. or early 62 A.D.

8. Philippians—written from Rome, 63 A.D.

9. I Timothy—written from north Greece (Macedonia) Perhaps Nicopolis. Late 63 A.D.

10. Titus—written about the same time as I Timothy.

11. II Timothy—written from Rome, late 67 A.D.